W9-BHX-770

DATE DUE

SEP 1 8 2008		
OCT 0 3 2008		
APR 0 7 2015		
1/9/16		
OCT 0 9 2019		

ME AND MY HORSE

Caring For My Horse

Toni Webber

COPPER BEECH BOOKS
Brookfield, Connecticut

© Aladdin Books Ltd 2002

Produced by:
Aladdin Books Ltd
28 Percy Street
London W1T 2BZ

ISBN 0–7613–2751–7

First published in the United States in 2002 by:
Copper Beech Books,
an imprint of
The Millbrook Press
2 Old New Milford Road
Brookfield, Connecticut 06804

Editor:
Harriet Brown

Designers:
Flick, Book Design & Graphics
Simon Morse

Illustrators:
James Field, Terry Riley, Stephen
Sweet, and Ross Watton—SGA
Frederick St. Ward

Cartoons: Simon Morse

Certain illustrations have
appeared in earlier books
created by Aladdin Books.

Printed in U.A.E.

Cataloging-in-Publication data is
on file at the Library of Congress.

Contents

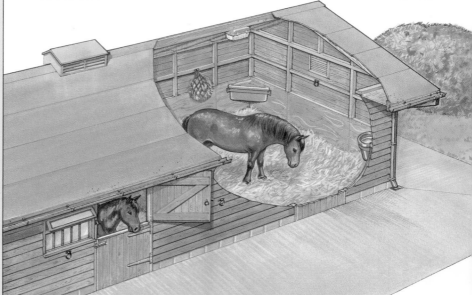

Introduction

Caring For My Horse is a lively guide to choosing a horse and taking care of its needs. There is much more to horses than simply riding them. They need a safe place to live, the right food and tack, and, importantly, they need you to look after their health. A happy, healthy, and well cared-for horse is much more enjoyable to ride and spend time with, whatever activities you choose to do together.

Follow Oscar and me as we get to know each other better —and do our best not to get into too much trouble.

Always Remember:

Look in these boxes for further information about looking after your horse. They contain important points that you should try to remember.

THE RIGHTS AND WRONGS

Watch for these check boxes, as they show you how to do things properly. Just as importantly, watch for the "X" boxes. These show you how not to do things.

Q What are these boxes for?

A These question and answer panels are here to help you with any questions you may have about looking after your horse. They are on subjects relevant to the rest of the page they're on.

Follow my horse diary to find out how I get along looking after my pony. Why not make your own horse diary to keep track of your progress? It will help you remember all the fun you have and all the new friends you make as you get to know your horse.

Choosing a horse

Owning a horse is something most riders dream about. It is also a big responsibility. There are many things to consider before you choose a horse. Where should you get it from? What sort of horse should it be? Where are you going to keep it? Here are some tips to help you choose the right horse.

Arab horse

BUY OR LEASE?

Getting a horse on lease means you don't have to begin spending a large amount of money. But its care is your responsibility just as much as if you had bought it. Do not forget that you will have to give the horse back one day.

English pony

WHICH HORSE?

A calm horse is best if you're a nervous rider. If you are experienced, you may want a horse that is more forward going. If the horse will be living in a field all year, a native breed would be a good choice. Don't buy a pony that you will quickly grow out of, or a big horse that you plan to "grow into."

13hh chestnut gelding. 9yrs. Excels XC 100% traffic, shoe, etc. $3,000

Q If I find a suitable horse, should I have it examined by a vet?

A It is usually best to get a horse examined. There are different levels of veterinary examinations. Expensive ones are detailed and include X rays. Cheaper ones simply tell you if the horse is fit enough for what you want it to do. Vetting can reveal a problem that means that the horse is not suitable to buy.

Q Should I get my horse insured?

A Yes, you should make sure that you are covered for any damage that your horse may cause to someone else. You can also insure your horse against injury, as vet's fees can be expensive, and for the loss of and damage to your tack.

UNDERSTANDING THE ADS

This ad tells you that the pony is a 9-year-old chestnut gelding (male), 13 hands high. He is good at cross-country, is safe on the road, and is easy to shoe. But there is a lot it doesn't say. For example, is he easy to catch? Make a list of questions to ask the seller.

ACTION

The way a horse moves makes a difference to its fitness, the way it handles, and how comfortable it is to ride. Ask an experienced person to look at the horse's action for you.

✔ GOOD CONFORMATION

Conformation means the way a horse is put together. The horse should look in good proportion and be alert. Its eyes should be large and set well apart. Its feet should point straight ahead and its quarters should be muscular and strong.

✗ Goose rump
The rump slopes steeply from the highest point of the quarters to the tail.

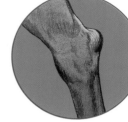

✗ Narrow chest
Its chest should be wide enough to give its heart plenty of room. But a very wide chest can cause it to be an uncomfortable ride.

✗ Capped hocks
Capped hocks look as though they are a serious fault, but they don't actually cause a problem for the horse.

quarters

✗ Splints
A splint is a bony swelling on the leg, usually below the knee. Once a splint has formed it is not a serious condition.

fetlock

✗ Windgalls
A windgall is a soft swelling just above the fetlock. This should not stop you from buying the horse as it is not a serious condition.

✗ Cracked hooves
A horse with brittle hooves might become lame and be difficult to shoe. Strong hooves often mean a healthy horse.

Always Remember:

Take a knowledgeable person with you when you go to look at a horse. Before you go, write down any questions that you need to ask. It is easy to forget questions when you get there. Try not to fall in love with the first horse you see—it is important to keep an open mind. It is a good idea to ask if you can have the horse for two weeks on a trial basis.

Saturday
We went to look at a pony today. She sounded lovely in the ad. The only thing was, she turned out to be just 9 hands high. As one hand is about 4 inches, she was really much too small for me!

The stall

Wednesday
Guess what! Mom has ended up buying me Oscar—he's my favorite pony at the riding stable. I still can't believe it. We are boarding him at the riding stable as we don't have a stall or field of our own. It means getting up really early so that I can do his stall before school, but it's worth it.

A stall is useful but not absolutely necessary in the care of a pony. It is more important in the care of a horse, and should be warm, light, and well drained.

STALL FITTINGS

The stall should be on level ground and have a split door so that your horse can look out. The roof should overhang the front of the stall to protect your horse from the weather. Windows should have bars over them and the floor should be made of concrete, with a built-in drain. Any lights must be out of reach of your horse.

N
E
W
S

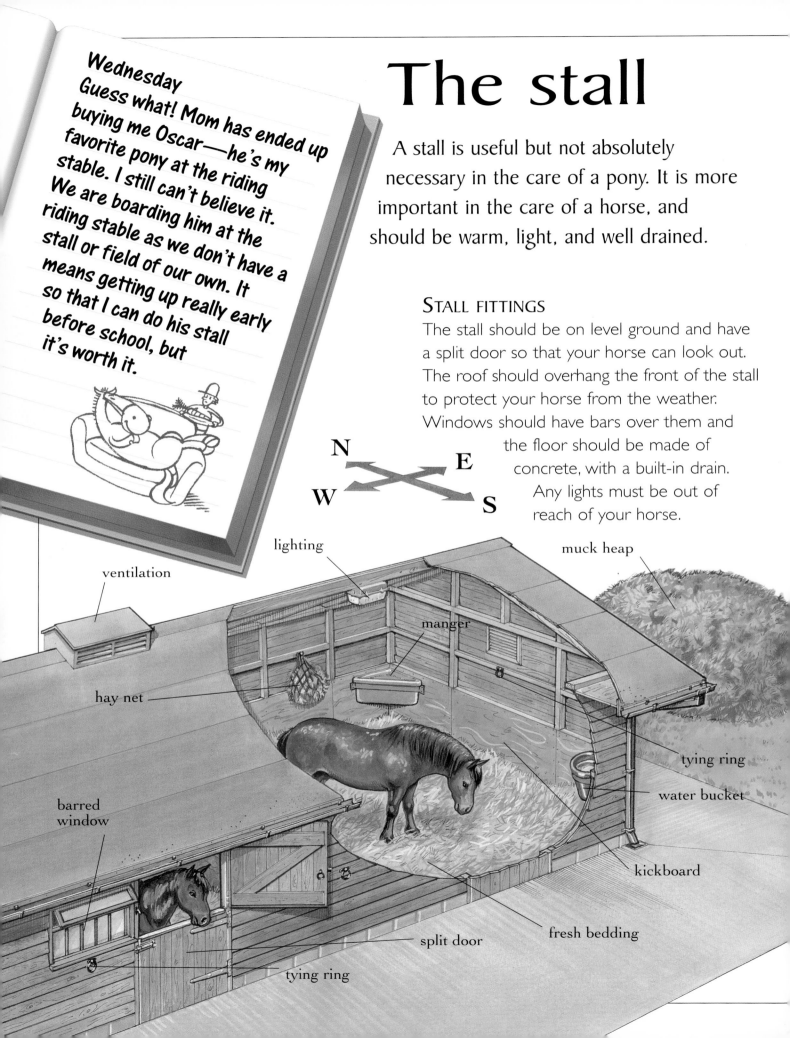

ventilation

lighting

muck heap

hay net

manger

barred window

tying ring

water bucket

kickboard

split door

fresh bedding

tying ring

LAYING BEDS AND MUCKING OUT

1 Every day, take all the droppings and wet bedding out of the stall using a fork and a manure bucket or a wheelbarrow. If you have time, sweep all the bedding to one side to allow the floor to dry.

2 Replace the wet bedding with fresh bedding.

When you lay a bed in an empty stall, use as much bedding as you can. Spread it over the floor to make a thick, soft layer. Make banks of bedding around the edges of the stall. Your horse needs less straw in the day than at night.

rake

manure fork

manure bucket

wheelbarrow

broom

shovel

1

2

Q What is the best bedding to use?

A Wood shavings are the most common bedding, but you must make sure there are no sharp splinters in it. Sawdust can be used with wood shavings, but it is dusty and can clog up drains. Straw is also generally used for bedding. Shredded paper is popular because it is warm and dust free. But it is also heavy when damp, and some horses may be allergic to the ink in the paper.

Straw

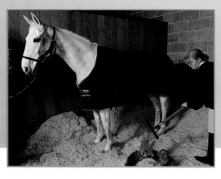

Wood shavings

Friday
I'm learning to give Oscar a really comfortable bed. At first, I didn't use enough bedding. Gerry, the owner of the riding stable, had to show me how much to use. She made me build really thick banks around the edges. I had to pat them with the back of my shovel to make them square.

Keeping a horse outdoors

Horses are grazing animals. If possible, fresh grass should always be part of their diet. In moderate climates, horses are healthier if they live outdoors even in winter. Even in harsher climates, horses may spend part of many days out in the field.

TYPES OF GRASS

Old, well-established pastureland is the best grazing for horses. Lots of different grasses will have grown over the years. New grass or grass that has been fertilized could be too rich for your horse.

Horsetail
This weed is most often found on waste ground. It can grow in fields where the grass hasn't been properly cared for.

POISONOUS PLANTS

Some plants are poisonous to horses. Check that there is nothing dangerous growing in or near your field. Ask an adult to help you pull up any dangerous plants and burn them on a bonfire.

White snakeroot
This plant grows on the edge of woodlands. It can be removed by using a herbicide (chemical).

Ragwort
This weed grows on vacant land and in fields. It should be pulled up by the roots and burned.

Deadly nightshade
This plant grows mainly in wooded areas, but should be pulled up if it grows in or near your horse's field.

Red maple
These trees should be fenced off from your horse's field.

CARE OF THE PASTURE

Horses and ponies waste a lot of grass in their field. They often trample good grass and turn other areas sour with their droppings. Pick up droppings every day using a shovel and a wheelbarrow.

Or you could use heavy waterproof gloves to pick up the droppings. It is a job well worth doing as it helps to keep the grass and your horse healthy.

RESTING FIELDS

If your riding stable has a lot of grazing land, it may be divided up into smaller fields. Fields that are empty for a while can be sprayed with pesticide (chemical) to get rid of parasites and weeds. Sheep or cattle can be kept in fields with horses. This improves the quality of the grazing since sheep and cattle eat grass that horses leave.

Bracken
This is found on vacant land and in woodland. Bracken is dangerous over a long period of time as it can damage your horse's liver.

Yew
Yew trees are extremely poisonous. If your horse's field borders land where yew trees grow, it is very important to fence them off. Every part of the tree is poisonous—even the twigs.

Black locust
This is found mainly by the side of the road. Your horse must not be allowed to eat it.

1 pm—Oscar was right at the far side of the field this morning. I had to trek through the mud to get him. Next week, he's going into one of the smaller paddocks so that the big field can be rested and given some fertilizer. He'll be with Annabel's pony, Daniel, so he won't get lonely.

Q Is it all right to keep my horse in a field by itself?

A Most horses do not like to be kept on their own. They are herd animals and need company. If there aren't any other horses to share your horse's field, you could put a few sheep, cows, or even a goat in the field.

Sunday
There was a dead bird in Oscar's water trough this morning. Ugh! I got it out and Annabel and I decided that the water might not be very good for the ponies to drink. So we had to empty the trough and clean it out. Now Oscar and Daniel have nice, clean water to drink.

Fencing

The fence around your field must be strong and well built. Inspect it regularly to check for any damage. It does not have to be very high, because even horses that are good at jumping rarely try to jump out. The gate also needs to be strong and easy for you—but not for your horse—to open and close.

TYPES OF FENCING

The best type of fence to use is a strongly built, wooden post-and-rail fence. Fences with three rails are the most popular. Another popular type of fence has plain wire or plastic in place of the wooden rails. Try to avoid barbed wire and wire netting because these can be dangerous for your horse.

✓ **Post and rail**
This is a safe and secure type of fence. Three rails are better than two.

✓ **Post and plastic rail**
Broad plastic strips are a cheaper alternative to wooden rails. Plastic strips are better than plain wire fencing because they are seen more easily.

✓ **Rail and wire**
The wire used in this type of fence must be plain, not barbed. It must also be pulled taut or your horse could get tangled in it.

Q What sort of gate is best for my horse's field?

A The best gate is a five-barred one, which swings open without touching the ground. It should have a latch that your horse cannot open. You can avoid damage to the gate by not climbing over it or sitting on it. If you must climb over it, always do so at the hinge end. Your gate must be wide enough for your horse to pass through easily.

FIELD SECURITY

You must make sure that the gate to your field is always securely shut. Some horses learn how to open gates, so you should fit a horse-proof latch. You could put on a padlock as a precaution against horse thieves. As a further guard, you could get your horse freeze-marked. This involves having your horse permanently marked with a number, usually on its back. If it is stolen and offered for sale, the number makes it easier for the police to know that the horse is yours.

FIELD SHELTER

Most horses don't mind bad weather as long as they have somewhere to shelter from the wind. The side of a building, a high hedge, or a hollow in the ground all offer shelter. A special run-in shelter can provide protection from wind and rain. In summer, your horse can use it to escape from flies and the hot sun.

prevailing wind

bedding

Always Remember:

Make sure that your horse has enough to drink. If you are lucky, water will be piped to a trough. These troughs are usually controlled by a valve so that they cannot overflow. Otherwise, you will have to fill your trough regularly using a hose. An old bathtub can be used as a water trough. Make sure that all the faucets have been taken off and that there are no sharp edges for your horse to injure itself on. In the winter you must break the ice in the trough every day.

Dual system

When you have both a stall and a field, you can give your horse the best of both worlds—living in and living out. This dual system is used by many riding stables and works very well.

Winter

Always Remember :

Lay a good, thick bed, especially on winter nights. A thick bed gives your horse a comfortable resting place if it wants to lie down. Some horses are very restless and paw at their bedding and create bare patches. All you can do is add as much bedding as you can. The daytime bed in summer does not need to be as thick as a nighttime or winter bed. Your horse is less likely to lie down during the day.

HALF IN, HALF OUT

Using the dual system means that your horse spends half the time indoors and half in the field. In the summer, it is best to keep your horse in the stall during the day and out in the field at night. In the winter, your horse is better off in the stall at night. It can go out in the field for exercise during daylight hours.

FULL LIVERY

Full livery is when you hand the daily care of your horse over to the riding stable. The owner of the stable makes sure that it is fed, has new shoes, and is wormed. Everything is done for you. It is not the most popular type of livery as you miss out on all the fun of caring for your horse.

PARTIAL LIVERY

With partial livery, you agree with the owner of the yard exactly how much time you can spend looking after your horse. The staff at the riding stable will do the rest. This could mean that you exercise and muck out every day, but the staff arranges shoeing, worming, and giving feeds at night.

ROUGH BOARD

The cost of rough board covers a stall and grazing for your horse. It should also include space in a hay store for your hay and space in the feed room for your horse's feed. Everything else is your responsibility.

Summer

TACK SECURITY

Tack security is very important. Tack thefts are common, and often the stolen property is not recovered. All your tack should be marked with your name and other identifying marks in permanent pen. Any other belongings that you leave at the stables—rugs, bandages, etc.— should carry identification. If you can, store your tack in a locked room. In some stables, security lights and guard dogs discourage thieves.

Later
The tack room at our stable is a sort of double room. The inside is like a big walk-in closet. It has a lock, and everyone keeps saddles and bridles in there. We have bridle hooks and saddle racks with our horses' names on them. In the outer room we keep things like rugs, hats, and grooming kits.

Grooming

Most horses enjoy being groomed—some even fall asleep while you work. Grooming keeps the skin healthy and the coat shiny. Daily grooming ensures that you notice any cuts or other problems as early as possible.

stable rubber

sponges

dandy brush

hoof oil and brush

hoof pick

body brush

water brush

curry comb (metal)

sweat scraper

curry comb (rubber)

mane comb

mane-pulling comb

QUICK-RELEASE KNOT

1

2

3

When tying a horse up, always use a quick-release knot, as shown on the left. It will hold your horse securely. To undo the knot, remove the loose end from the loop and tug it sharply. A quick-release knot like this may be necessary if your horse gets tangled up in any way.

PICKING OUT HOOVES

Cleaning out your horse's hooves is something you should never forget to do. Work from the back of the foot toward the toe using a metal hoof pick. Pay special attention to the grooves on each side of the center "V" of the foot, called the frog.

Grooming kit
To make sure you don't lose any items in your grooming kit, keep them all together in a grooming box. If your horse is at a livery stable, write your name or your horse's name on each piece of equipment.

Always Remember:

Attach a loop of baler twine to each metal tie ring in your stall. Tie your horse to the twine, not to the metal ring. If your horse is frightened and pulls back suddenly, the twine will break and your horse will not injure itself. Your hay net should also be tied to a baler twine loop.

ORDER OF GROOMING

The usual order of grooming is to work from the top of the head to the hindquarters. Do this first on one side and then on the other. Use the body brush to brush the head, mane, and tail. Finish off the body with the stable rubber. Sponge the eyes, nose, and dock area (under the tail).

PULLING THE MANE

You only need to pull your horse's mane if it is very thick or tangled. The purpose is to shorten it, make it lie flat, or make it easier to braid. Wrap a few hairs at a time around a comb and pull them out. Only pull the long hairs from underneath.

6.30 pm—I think Oscar must look for the muddiest part of the field before getting down to roll. I always seem to work harder than anyone else at getting him clean. I am just thankful that he isn't a gray. Getting rid of grass stains takes forever!

Q Is grooming a grass-kept horse any different from grooming a stabled horse?

A With a grass-kept horse, you can use a dandy brush directly on the coat. If your horse is very muddy, you can use a plastic or rubber curry comb on it. Take care not to groom a grass-kept horse too vigorously as it needs the natural grease in its coat to keep it warm and dry. Never pull a grass-kept horse's tail as it needs a full tail for protection from flies and the weather.

Use a dandy brush to remove mud from a grass-kept horse.

Use a body brush or an old, soft dandy brush on the tail—never use a mane comb.

OILING HOOVES

Your horse will look very sharp when its hooves are oiled. This is nearly always done before a show. Be careful not to oil the hooves too often. Spreading a thin film of oil over them stops them from absorbing water. This can make them brittle.

Use separate, differently colored sponges for the head and dock areas.

Pick out your horse's feet every day.

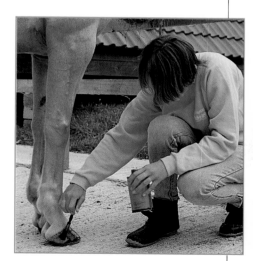

Tack

There are so many different items of tack that you may find it difficult to know what is best for your horse. Always ask for help from someone who really understands what each item is used for. It is very important to look after your tack properly.

Q How often should I clean my tack?

A If you want to be a perfectionist, the answer is every time you use it. This may be unrealistic, but you should aim to clean it once a week. It helps if you can rinse the bit and wipe mud from the tack after every ride. Inspect your saddle and bridle for damage each time you clean them.

TYPES OF GIRTH

The most popular girth is made of synthetic fabric and has a soft, strong filling. Other girths are made from leather, webbing, or string. Leather girths need a lot of care to keep them supple. String girths can pinch your horse.

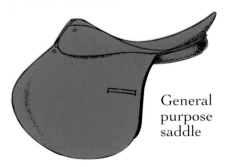

General purpose saddle

STIRRUP IRONS

Stirrup irons should be made from stainless steel. They must be large enough to leave about ¹/2 in (1 cm) clear on either side of your boot at its widest part. If they are bigger, your whole foot could slip through. If they are smaller, your foot could get stuck.

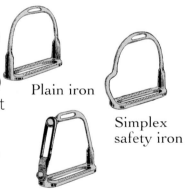

Plain iron

Simplex safety iron

Safety iron

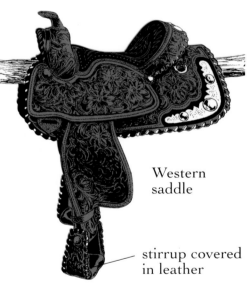

Western saddle

stirrup covered in leather

Always Remember:

Make sure that the hairs on your horse's back lie the right way under the saddle. To do this, place the saddle well up on the withers and push it back into place. If you use a numnah (a cloth under the saddle), it should be slightly bigger than the saddle, and must not press on the horse's backbone.

withers

numnah

TYPES OF SADDLE

General-purpose saddles are the most widely used. These are usually made of leather and are shaped to encourage the rider to sit in a balanced position. Western saddles are very comfortable for both the rider and the horse.

PUTTING ON THE BRIDLE

The main purpose of the bridle is to hold the bit in the correct position in your horse's mouth. The browband holds the headpiece in place behind your horse's ears. The cheekpieces can be adjusted to raise or lower the bit in the mouth. The throatlatch, which is part of the headpiece, prevents the bridle from coming off. The reins link the rider to the bit. Always loop the reins over your horse's neck when you put the bridle on.

Hold the headpiece with your right hand. Lift it to the level of your horse's ears. Give the bit to your horse with your left hand.

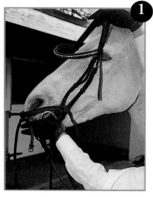

As soon as the bit is in your horse's mouth, put the headpiece over its ears.

Do up the throatlatch. There should be room for one hand's width between it and your horse's jawbone.

Do up the noseband. You should be able to insert two fingers between it and your horse's face.

Pelham bridle

NOSEBANDS

A simple noseband (or cavesson) is just for show as it is not needed to keep the bridle on. A drop

Drop noseband

noseband is used to stop a horse from opening its mouth so wide that the bit has no effect. Grakle nosebands work in the same way as a drop noseband. They have two nosebands, which cross over at the front.

Grakle noseband

TYPES OF BIT

The most common bit is the jointed snaffle. It presses on the corners of the mouth and the tongue. A curb bit has a curb chain. Pressure on the reins causes the curb chain to tighten in the chin groove to make your horse bring its nose in. A Pelham bit combines the actions of a curb bit and a snaffle bit.

Jointed snaffle bit

Pelham bit

curb chain

Curb bit

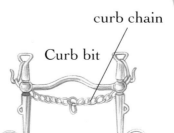

Mom bought me some second-hand stirrup leathers. They've been looked after so well that they're lovely and soft!

17

Friday
Oscar is so greedy I'm surprised he doesn't get a stomachache. He always finishes his feed before any of the other ponies. I am now adding more chaff to his feed to make him take a bit longer over eating it. So far it seems to be working. Annabel's pony, Daniel, finished first today.

Feeding

In the wild, horses and ponies find their food wherever they can. They cover large areas of land as they search for food. The food they find is quite varied—from sweet meadow grasses to the leaves and bark of trees. The variety gives them all the vitamins and minerals they need to stay healthy. Your horse, however, relies on you to control its diet.

Q What is hard food ?

Chaff and molasses meal

A Hard food is another name for concentrated food. Oats are the best all-around food but may be too rich for some horses. Barley is less rich than oats and is very useful for horses that lose weight easily. Cubes (pellets) or mixed food can be given instead of the actual grain. In both cases, the manufacturer uses different grains and a careful balance of vitamins and minerals in the feed. Ask an experienced person to help you choose the right feed for your horse.

Corn

Bran

Barley

Dried alfalfa

Grass

Hay

BULK FEED

The basis of a horse's diet is bulk food, such as grass and hay. The choice of any additional food you give your horse depends on the work it does and the type of horse it is. A very active horse needs a diet made up of 60% bulk food and 40% hard food. A horse that is out in a field as a break from normal work needs a diet of just bulk food. Ask an experienced person what the balance should be for your horse.

Winter feeding

14 hh pony 825 lb (375 kg) Stabled, hacking, some jumping. **FEED 19.5 lb (9 kg) per day**	8 a.m.	Noon	4 p.m.	8 p.m.
	2 lb (1 kg) hard food 4.5 lb (2 kg) hay	No hard food 2 lb (1 kg) hay	4.5 lb (2 kg) hard food No hay	No hard food 6.5 lb (3 kg) hay
12 hh pony 660 lb (300 kg) In at night, out during the day. Light hacking. **FEED 16 lb (7.4 kg) per day**	No hard food 4.5 lb (2 kg) hay in field	No hard food No hay	2 lb (1 kg) hard food 2 lb (1 kg) hay	No hard food 7.5 lb (3.4 kg) hay

Summer feeding

14 hh pony 825 lb (375 kg) Stabled daytime, out at night. Hacking, shows. **FEED 19.5 lb (9 kg) per day**	8 a.m.	Noon	4 p.m.	8 p.m.
	4.5 lb (2 kg) hard food 6.5 lb (3 kg) hay	No hard food No hay	2 lb (1 kg) hard food No hay	Turn out to pasture; grass is remainder of ration
12 hh pony 660 lb (300 kg) Out all the time. Light work, some shows. **FEED 16 lb (7kg) per day**	2 lb(1 kg) hard food No hay	Grass makes up rest of daily ration	Grass makes up rest of daily ration	Grass makes up rest of daily ration

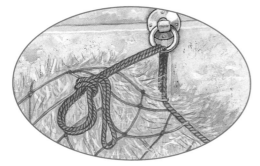

HAY

The customary hay for horses is meadow hay. Alfalfa (lucerne) is similar to hay. It contains lots of calcium, so horses fed on alfalfa need a smaller amount of hard food. You should feed hay in a hay net that is tied with a quick-release knot.

FEED QUANTITY

The chart above gives you an idea of what to feed two ponies of different heights and living arrangements. No two horses are the same. Some put on weight much more easily than others. Whatever your feeding routine, you must always provide fresh water for your horse.

I still can't believe how much water Oscar can drink— especially when we come back from a fast ride!

Tack and feed rooms

Tack is valuable and should be cared for properly. Regular cleaning is only one part of its care. The way it is stored is also important. In a well-run livery stable, the tack room sometimes feels like a meeting place when everyone is in there looking after their tack.

I have put up some extra hooks next to my saddle rack for my spare stirrup irons. They may come in handy one day.

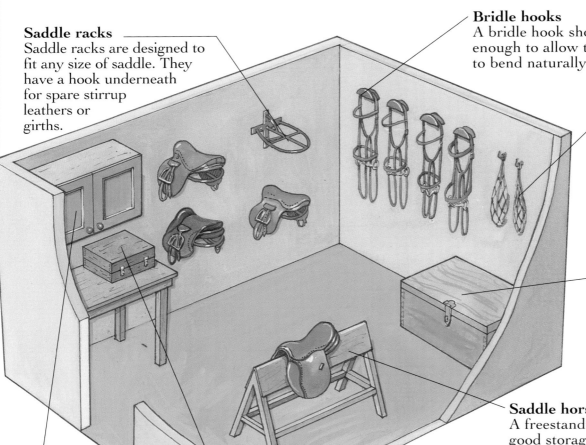

Saddle racks
Saddle racks are designed to fit any size of saddle. They have a hook underneath for spare stirrup leathers or girths.

Bridle hooks
A bridle hook should be wide enough to allow the headpiece to bend naturally over it.

Hay nets
Spare hay nets can be kept in the tack room if there is enough room for them.

Chest for rugs
A big, deep, dry chest is excellent for storing rugs that are not in use.

Saddle horse
A freestanding saddle rack is a good storage place for a spare saddle until it is provided with its own rack.

Medicine chest
A basic veterinary chest should contain antiseptic solution, nonadhesive dressings, a roll of adhesive tape, scissors, a poultice, and clean cotton balls.

Grooming box
Most horses have their own grooming kit. A kit normally contains dandy, body, and water brushes, a curry comb, hoof pick, sponges, and a stable rubber.

TACK ROOM
It is amazing how much equipment one horse can have. It is best to store your saddle on a shaped rack. Only store one saddle per rack. Your bridle should be kept on a proper bridle hook. Nails are good for storing girths, stirrup leathers, and head collars.

HANDLING AND CARRYING TACK

Treating your saddle carelessly could damage it. Inside a saddle is a framework called a tree. If you drop the saddle, you could break the tree. Trees cannot be repaired. To carry your saddle, let it rest over your forearm. Loop the bridle over your shoulder, with the reins caught up by the throatlatch. Never let the reins drag on the ground. Clean your tack regularly with saddle soap and a little water.

Q What should be kept in a feed room?

A The feed room should contain feed buckets, a wooden spoon for stirring, scoops for measuring, and scales for weighing. Hard food should be kept in vermin-proof bins with lids. Each type of food should be kept in a separate container and be labeled clearly. Vegetables should be stored off the ground.

STORAGE OF HAY

Hay should be stored in a proper haystore or barn. This protects it from the weather. The hay bales should be stacked on wooden pallets which keep them off the ground and allow air to circulate. If you must store them outdoors, you must put a waterproof cover over them that cannot blow off.

Monday
I decided to clean out my grooming box because it was really messy. Some hoof oil had been spilled, and it was all mixed up with braiding bands and an old hair net I thought I'd lost. It took me half an hour to clean the box properly. Oscar won't even notice!

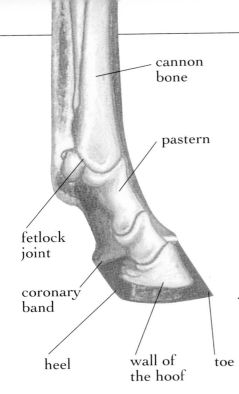

cannon bone

pastern

fetlock joint

coronary band

heel

wall of the hoof

toe

Feet and shoes

There is a saying, "No foot, no horse," and this is very true. A horse's feet need special care if it is to be healthy and capable of work. Hooves grow all the time, like fingernails. A good farrier will make sure that your horse has healthy feet and shoes that fit properly. Shoes stop your horse's feet from wearing down too fast when it is ridden on hard surfaces.

THE FOOT

Underneath your horse's foot you will see a soft V-shape, which extends from the heel toward the toe. This is the frog. It absorbs shock and improves the circulation of blood in the foot. The bars and the wall of the hoof give the foot strength. Your horse has no feeling in this part of its hoof, so it does not hurt your horse to have nails put in to keep the shoes on.

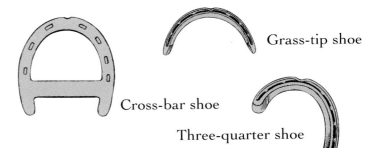

Grass-tip shoe

Cross-bar shoe

Three-quarter shoe

TYPES OF SHOE

Horseshoes are made of iron and have a groove in them to stop the horse from slipping. Cross-bar shoes and three-quarter shoes are used on horses with damaged feet. Grass-tip shoes are used on horses living out and not being ridden, to give protection to the front part of the foot.

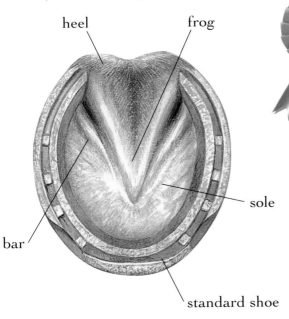

heel

frog

sole

bar

standard shoe

Always Remember:

Check and clean out your horse's feet every day. You need a hoof pick to remove mud and stones that get packed into the hollows between the frog and the wall. Use the hoof pick from the heel to the toe of each foot in turn. Sweep up the pickings afterward. You can paint the outside of the hoof with hoof oil to make your horse's feet look sharp. It is a good idea to carry a hoof pick in your pocket when out riding. You never know when you might need it.

FOOT PROBLEMS

Some foot problems can be remedied by changing your horse's diet. Others need the attention of a good farrier. Sand cracks are cracks that run down from the top of the hoof. They are a serious condition. Grass cracks run upward from the ground and are less serious. If you are unsure of what to do about a foot problem, ask your farrier for advice.

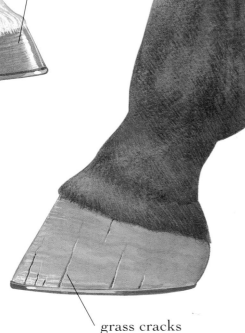

healthy foot

grass cracks

Q How often should the farrier tend my horse?

A You will need to call the farrier every four to eight weeks. Check your horse's shoes daily. If the hoof wall sticks out over the shoe, the foot needs trimming. Other signs that your horse needs new shoes include: the shoes clicking, your horse stumbling a lot, clenches (risen nails) sticking up from the wall of the hoof, thin shoes, and loose shoes.

TYPES OF STUD

There are two types of stud—the road stud and the competition stud. Both give your horse extra grip. Studs are only used in the hind shoes. Road studs are shallow with a hard tip. Competition studs are pointed, for use in hard, dry conditions, or large and square, for use in mud.

Road stud   Competition stud

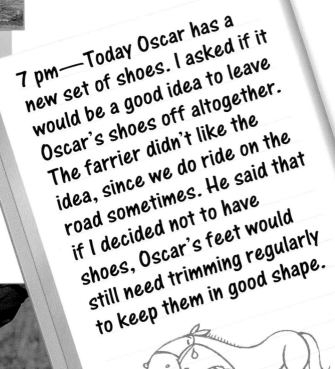

7 pm—Today Oscar has a new set of shoes. I asked if it would be a good idea to leave Oscar's shoes off altogether. The farrier didn't like the idea, since we do ride on the road sometimes. He said that if I decided not to have shoes, Oscar's feet would still need trimming regularly to keep them in good shape.

Health check

Your horse cannot tell you if it is feeling ill. It is up to you to recognize signs of sickness and be ready to obtain a treatment or call a vet. Luckily, most horses and ponies remain healthy and are usually fit and active well into old age.

HEAD CHECK

A healthy horse's eyes are wide open and bright. Its ears should be pricked and it should be alert. The nostrils should be free from discharge. Breathing should be quiet and even. A sick horse will seem listless and dull eyed. It will show little interest in its surroundings. There could be discharge from its eyes or nose.

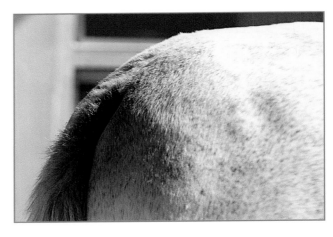

COAT CHECK

A healthy horse has a sleek, flat coat and supple skin. Horses can get a condition called sweet itch (above). They get so itchy that they can rub all the hair from their tail or mane. If your horse's coat is dull and it seems to be sweating, then there may be something wrong. If there is no experienced person around to advise you, always call the vet.

3 pm—Oscar seemed a bit lame today. When we looked him over, we couldn't find anything wrong. His legs weren't hot or swollen, and he hadn't gotten a stone in his shoe. He must have stepped on something sharp. We're going to give him a rest tomorrow and see how he is the next day.

Always Remember:

Check for saddle or girth galls if your horse is overweight or has not been ridden for a while. These are small, painful swellings on the skin that form under the saddle and girth. This mainly happens in the spring, when horses eat lots of new grass and put on weight. The condition is made worse by badly-fitting or dirty tack. If the skin is broken, bathe it gently in a mild antiseptic solution. Do not use the saddle on the horse until the sores have completely healed.

Q Do I need to vaccinate my horse?

A Yes. Vaccination will protect your horse against equine flu and an illness called tetanus. It also may not be able to go to some shows and competitions without a valid vaccination certificate.

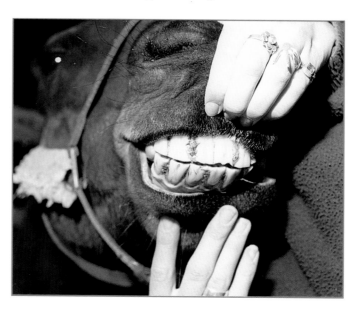

Later
Oscar had his flu shot today. It was really amazing. The vet just patted him on the neck, talking to him all the time, and the next thing I knew he was screwing a syringe into the needle that was sticking into Oscar's neck. I don't think Oscar felt a thing.

GENERAL HEALTH

Horses are generally healthy and are rarely ill. If a horse is limping, the cause is most likely to be in the foot, but you should check the lower legs for heat or swelling. You can apply a poultice to reduce swelling, but lameness usually is treated by rest.

Listlessness
This is a sign that something is wrong. Your horse will hang its head. Its eyes and coat will look dull. It will have no interest in what is going on.

Lameness
Check that nothing is stuck in the foot. Rest is the best cure for lameness.

Off feed
This could mean your horse has an internal problem. Drinking much more water than normal can also mean that something is wrong.

TEETH CHECK

Your horse's teeth continue to grow throughout its life. The front teeth are used to pull grass or hay. The back teeth grind the food before it is swallowed. Sometimes, the teeth develop sharp edges. Occasionally a back tooth will grow so long that it damages the tongue and the inside of the cheek. Your horse should have a regular visit from the horse dentist so that its teeth can be rasped (have sharp edges removed).

Protective clothing

We expect our horses to do things they would never do in the wild. We clip their coats and take them traveling, pull their manes and tails, and teach them to jump. It is only fair that you protect your horse from injury by providing it with rugs, bandages, and other forms of clothing.

BLANKETS

One popular blanket is the New Zealand rug. It is designed to be warm and waterproof and will not slip even if your horse is galloping in a field. If your horse is stabled, it needs a night blanket and a wool or quilted day blanket. These are not waterproof. Antisweat sheets prevent chills and are used on a sweaty horse. In warm weather, a summer sheet provides protection against flies. All blankets must fit properly.

LEG BANDAGES

There are two types of leg bandage—the stable bandage and the exercise bandage. Stable bandages are usually made from wool. They are used with some form of padding to make cold, wet legs warm and dry. It is important not to put the bandage on too tightly— you could damage the leg. Exercise bandages are slightly elasticized and are also used with padding. They support the leg, but should not be left on longer than necessary.

Thursday
I asked Gerry, who owns the stable, whether Oscar should have a New Zealand rug. She said that as he was a hardy Dartmoor pony, he did not need one. I think she's right because she has other English ponies. None of them wears a rug and they're all very healthy.

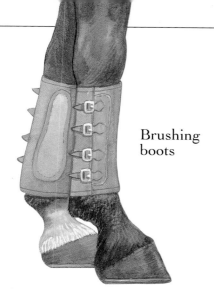

Brushing boots

Overreach boots

BOOTS

Brushing boots protect the leg from being injured by the opposite leg. They are fastened with leather or velcro straps. Fetlock boots, kneecaps, and hock boots are all designed to protect the joints. Overreach boots are bell-shaped and made of rubber. They cover the hoof and prevent the heels of the front feet from being damaged by the hind hooves.

TAIL BANDAGE

Tail bandages help to keep the top of the tail neat and tidy during travel. Wrap it around the tail from as high up the dock (the area at the top of your horse's tail) as possible. When you get to the end of the tail bone, tie it in place. Don't put it on too tightly or leave it on for any longer than necessary. To remove it, hold it at the top and pull it downward.

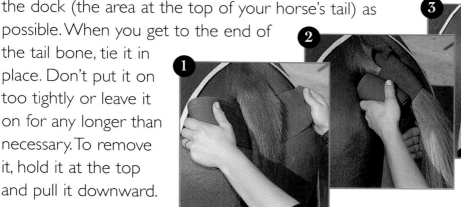

TRAVELING

When traveling in a horse trailer, your horse needs protection from bumps. It should wear a lightweight blanket, even in warm weather. Fit a tail guard over the tail bandage. This attaches to the back of the rug with straps. Traveling boots protect the legs from just above the knee to the top of the hoof. They should be removed as soon as the trip is over. If your horse is likely to throw its head up, you can protect the top of its head with a poll guard. This fastens to the head collar.

Sunday
Gerry took us to a forest for a change of scenery. She loaded the ponies into a horse trailer and off we went. We had a great time. Gerry loaned me some traveling boots for Oscar. They made him walk strangely —it was so funny!

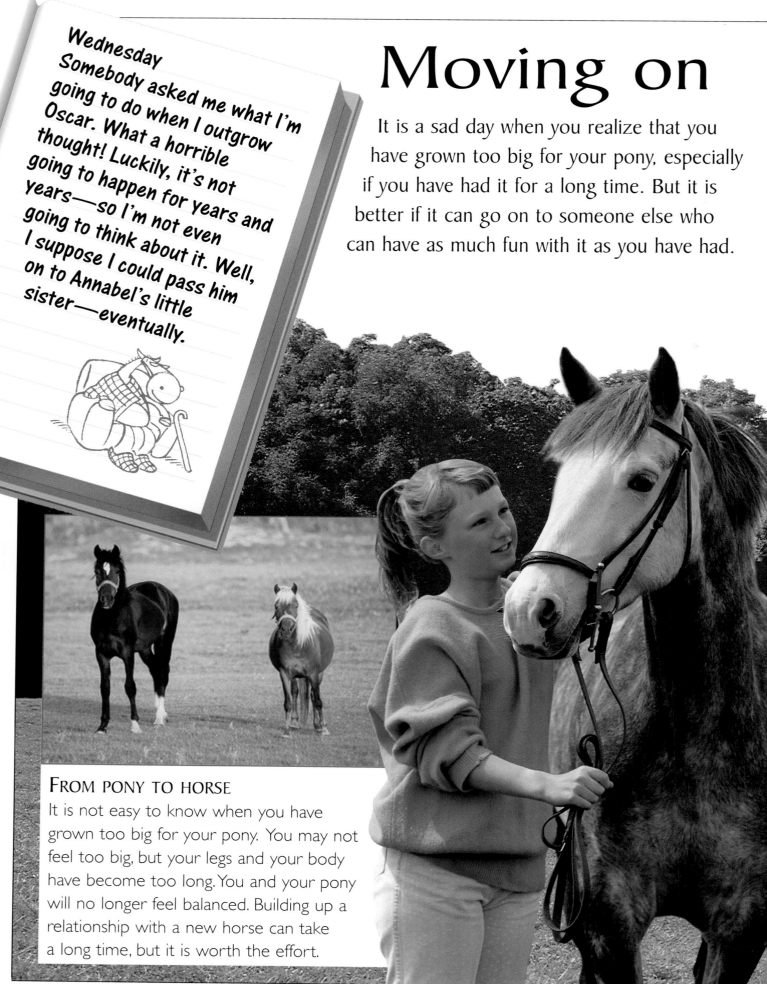

Moving on

It is a sad day when you realize that you have grown too big for your pony, especially if you have had it for a long time. But it is better if it can go on to someone else who can have as much fun with it as you have had.

Wednesday
Somebody asked me what I'm going to do when I outgrow Oscar. What a horrible thought! Luckily, it's not going to happen for years and years—so I'm not even going to think about it. Well, I suppose I could pass him on to Annabel's little sister—eventually.

FROM PONY TO HORSE

It is not easy to know when you have grown too big for your pony. You may not feel too big, but your legs and your body have become too long. You and your pony will no longer feel balanced. Building up a relationship with a new horse can take a long time, but it is worth the effort.

RETIREMENT

An old pony may not be very agile or fast but it can still easily carry children on its back. The ideal retirement for a pony is for it to remain in familiar surroundings with its old companions. It can still do a little regular work to keep fit.

Q What choices do I have when I outgrow my pony?

A You could put your pony out on loan. If it is a good pony, there will be no shortage of volunteers. You may have to sell your pony in order to buy a new horse. Don't worry, it can be just as happy in its next home as it was with you. If you have a younger brother or sister, you could pass your pony on to him or her.

Evening—We are all so sad. Nipper has been put to sleep. He was Gerry's first pony and she had him for 25 years. He'd been really miserable recently, off his food and drinking a lot, so Gerry got the vet to come and look at him. There was nothing the vet could do to help him. Gerry was so upset, but we comforted her by pointing out that Nipper had had a wonderful life.

THE END OF ITS LIFE

Some horses live well into their twenties, thirties, or even forties. However, it is not kind to prolong the life of a horse or pony that is constantly in pain. If your horse is no longer enjoying life, then it should be put to sleep. It is kinder and more humane for this to be done at home in familiar surroundings. Your vet will advise you of the best method and will carry it out with sympathy and understanding.

Quiz time

Can you remember what you have learned in this book? Test yourself and your friends by trying this quiz.

I What name is given to each of the following?
  a A steeply sloping rump
  b A soft swelling just above the fetlock
  c A bony swelling below the knee

2 Name four types of bedding.

3 What do we call:
  a The fleshy V-shaped section on the bottom of the foot?
  b The cloth that goes under the saddle?
  c The tools used for getting mud off a field-kept horse?

4 Name four poisonous plants.

5 Name four types of rug.

6 What are:
  a Brushing boots?
  b Overreach boots?
  c Traveling boots?

7 Give four signs of illness.

8 Name two types of noseband that are used to stop a horse from opening its mouth too wide.

Useful addresses

USA Pony Clubs
4041 Iron Works
  Parkway
Lexington, KY 40511-8462
www.ponyclub.org
Tel: (859) 254-7669

USA Equestrian, Inc.
4047 Iron Works
  Parkway
Lexington, KY 40511-8463
www.equestrian.org
Tel: (859) 254-2476

Saturday
I've been thinking it's about time Oscar and I got a bit more ambitious. I might enter some shows with him next summer. Gymkhana games would be fun!

Answers
1 a Goose rump b Windgall c Splint 2 Straw, shavings, sawdust, shredded paper 3 a Frog b Numnah c Dandy brush and curry comb 4 Choose from yew, ragwort, bracken, acorns, horse tail, deadly nightshade, black locust, white snakeroot 5 New Zealand rug, sweat rug, summer sheet, day rug 6 a Wrap-around leg guards b Bell-shaped rubber boots that fit over the front feet c Leg wraps, usually made of quilted material, that reach from above the knee or hock to the hoof 7 Listlessness, sweating, off feed, discharge from nostrils 8 Drop noseband and grakle noseband

Glossary

alfalfa
A plant used for making hay, also known as lucerne. It is very rich in calcium.

bars
Ridges underneath the hoof on either side of the frog.

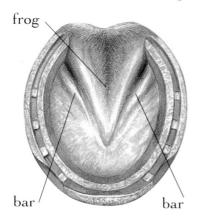

frog

bar   bar

clenches
Horseshoe nails after they have passed through the hoof and the tops of them have been twisted off.

coronary band
The top of the hoof from which the horn of the hoof grows.

dock
The area under a horse's tail.

farrier
A trained person who takes care of a horse's feet and fits new shoes.

frog
The V-shaped part of the underneath of the hoof. It absorbs shock.

gelding
A male horse or pony that is suitable for riding. A female is called a mare.

girth
The strap that holds the saddle in place on a horse.

hands
Horses and ponies are measured in hands. It is a unit of measurement that is roughly the width of an adult's hand. One hand is equal to 4 inches (10 cm).

livery
The name given to the practice of keeping a horse at a stall that isn't your own. You pay a fee to the owner of the stable.

manure bucket
A container used to collect dirt and droppings that have been picked up from a stall or field.

rasping
When a vet removes sharp edges from the teeth of a horse.

studs
Metal bolts that screw into a horse's shoes to give it extra grip on slippery ground.

sweet itch
A severe skin condition that affects the top of the tail and the crest of the neck. The horse gets very itchy and can rub off all its hair.

trough
A large container used to hold drinking water for horses in a field.

vetting
When a vet checks the health of a horse or pony.

withers
The projecting bone at the base of the neck. The height of a horse is measured from here.

worming
When you give a horse treatment to get rid of worms living in the horse's gut. Treatment may be a paste squirted into the mouth or a powder mixed with feed.